GET $mart WITH YOUR MONEY™

Smart **Saving** and **Financial Planning**

Carla Mooney

ROSEN
PUBLISHING®

New York

Published in 2013 by The Rosen Publishing Group, Inc.
29 East 21st Street, New York, NY 10010

Library of Congress Cataloging-in-Publication Data

Mooney, Carla, 1970–
Smart savings and financial planning/Carla Mooney.—1st ed.
    p. cm.—(Get smart with your money)
Includes bibliographical references and index.
ISBN 978-1-4488-8251-9 (library binding)—
ISBN 978-1-4488-8258-8 (pbk.)—
ISBN 978-1-4488-8259-5 (6-pack)
1. Finance, Personal. 2. Savings accounts. I. Title.
HG179.M59956 2013
332.024—dc23

2012024917

Manufactured in the United States of America

CPSIA Compliance Information: Batch #W13YA: For further information, contact Rosen Publishing, New York, New York, at 1-800-237-9932.

Contents

Introduction

Saving money is a smart choice for your financial future. Saving today will enable you to buy the things you want in the future. Maybe you want to go to college. Perhaps you want to buy a new car. You may need to replace an obsolete computer or another piece of electronic equipment. To pay for these things, you can take control of your money and learn how to make smart saving and spending choices.

Some people spend all the money they make on things they enjoy today, without thinking of what they may want or need in the future. If you spend impulsively, you may not have the money for the things you want. For some, spending without thought leads to debt. And debt is a slippery slope that you must be careful to avoid.

Saving and financial planning are important steps for your financial future. Saving increases your wealth and net worth. Plan for tomorrow by setting goals for what you want to achieve. Do you want to take a vacation or buy something big like a motorcycle? These are goals that you can reach by saving and financial planning. Small, regular savings can grow into a big account over the years. The sooner you start to save and invest, the longer your money has to earn interest and grow. In

Teens can use saving strategies and financial planning to help them meet financial goals. This teen is using money that he has saved to purchase a car.

this way, smart saving decisions today will make more money for you tomorrow.

The first step in savings and financial planning is to understand your current financial position. How much money do you have, how much do you earn, and how much are you spending? With this information, you can paint a complete picture of your financial standing today. Then you can create a path to carry you toward your future goals.

As you work toward your goals, creating a budget and savings plan will give you the tools you need to make smart spending and savings choices. These tools are key components to managing your money responsibly. You know where you are today and what your goals are for the future. Setting a budget and sticking to it shows you how your decisions affect your finances. Learning how to develop and use a savings plan will give you the roadmap to reach your goals.

Without smart savings and financial planning, you might find yourself making day-to-day money choices that leave you without money for the things you really want. What seems like a good purchase today may not make sense when you realize what you will have to give up tomorrow. Using smart savings and financial planning, you can take control of your money and feel confident about your future.

Chapter 1

Getting Started Saving

Saving money might not be as fun as spending money, but it is important to do. When you save money, you can use it later to buy things that you want, like video games and clothes. You might save enough to pay for larger things, like college or a car.

Saving is amazing! Small, regular savings can grow into a big account over the years. People who put a small amount of money into a savings account as often as they can and leave it untouched may be amazed at how big the account grows. How does this happen? Smart savers use interest and the magic of compounding to make their savings grow.

The Magic of Interest—Simple and Compound

When you put your money in a savings account at a bank and leave it there, the bank will pay you interest to use your money. Banks pay interest as a percentage of the money in your account. For example, a bank may pay 2 percent interest annually (each year) on money in

savings accounts. If you have $1,000 in your account, you will earn $20 in interest at the end of the year.

There are two basic ways to calculate interest: simple interest and compound interest. Simple interest is calculated as a flat percentage on your initial savings. Your initial savings is the money you place in an account. It is also called your principal.

Simple interest is calculated as follows:

Principal * Interest Rate = Interest

If you have $1,000 in a bank account and the interest rate is 5 percent, the simple interest you would earn on your principal is:

$1,000 * .05 = $50

Most of the time, interest is compounded. Compounding means that as you earn interest on your savings, it is added to your initial savings. Then you earn interest on the interest you have already earned. Interest can be compounded annually, monthly, or daily. The more often compounding occurs, the faster your money grows.

To calculate compounded interest, you can use this formula:

V = P (1+R/F)FY

Where:
V = Total value
P = Initial savings or principal
R = Interest rate
F = Frequency (how often interest is calculated each year)
Y = Number of years

There are also many interest calculators online that you can use.

In our example, assume that your savings of $1,000 earns 5 percent interest, compounded monthly. At the end of one year, you will have earned:

$$V = \$1,000\ (1+.05/12)12*1$$
$$V = \$1,000\ (1 + 0.0042)12$$
$$V = \$1,000 * 1.004212$$
$$V = \$1,000 * 1.052$$
$$V = \$1,052$$

When you open a savings account with your local bank, you can earn interest on the money in the account. A representative at the bank will assist you in opening the account.

At first, the difference between simple and compounded interest may seem tiny. However, compounding can really add up over a long period. In our example, assume your $1,000 principal earns 5 percent interest, compounded monthly. After twenty years, your investment would grow as follows:

$$V = \$1,000(1+.05/12)12*5$$
$$V = \$1,000(1 + 0042)60$$
$$V = \$1,000 * 1.004260$$
$$V = \$1,000 * 2.734$$
$$V = \$2,734$$

At the end of twenty years, your savings will have grown to $2,730 without you adding another penny to it. This is why people call it the magic of compounding!

Understanding how to calculate interest on the money in your savings account will help you determine how long it will take your savings to grow.

Rule of 72

There is a quick way to figure out how long it will take your savings to double. It is called the Rule of 72.

Calculate the Rule of 72 as follows (assume interest compounds annually):

72 / Interest rate = Number of years it will take for your savings to double

For example, if you have your money in a bank account paying 5 percent interest, you can make the following quick calculation: 72 / 5 = 14.4. It will take a little more than fourteen years for your money to double.

You can also use the Rule of 72 to estimate the interest rate you will need in order for your money to double in a specific number of years. For example, if you want your money to double in ten years, you can do a quick calculation: 72 / 10 = 7.2. You would need to earn 7.2 percent interest on your savings to double your money in ten years.

Understanding Net Worth

The first step to smart saving and financial planning is to figure out where you are today. A net worth statement is a financial snapshot at a point in time. It lists everything you own that has monetary value, which are your assets. It also lists everything you owe, like credit card balances or a car loan. These debts are your liabilities.

Net worth statements are valuable tools that help you on your way to smart saving and financial planning. A net worth statement can help you set the financial goals you want to work toward. It helps you assess how much progress you have

Inflation Danger

Inflation is an increase in the price you pay for goods. When you save money over a long period, you risk losing buying power if inflation makes prices rise quickly. For example, if a television costs $500 in year one, a 5 percent inflation rate would make the same television cost $525 in year two. When saving for a long-term goal, you need to consider inflation and how it will affect the amount of money you will need to meet your goal. Inflation rates change based on the economy. In 2011, the annual inflation rate was 3.16 percent. In the early 1980s, however inflation soared to 10 to 13 percent annually. If your financial goals are several years in the future, it is important to consider inflation in your plans.

made toward your goals. It can show you where you may need to adjust your plans. If you plan to apply for a mortgage, car loan, or credit card, lenders may ask to see your net worth statement.

How to Prepare Your Net Worth Statement

To prepare a net worth statement, start by listing your assets. Your assets may include things like bank accounts, investments, a car, jewelry, a house, or electronics. Then give each item a dollar value. If you have bank accounts or investments,

you should receive statements monthly or quarterly that show the current value of your account. For items like electronics, cars, and jewelry, you want to use fair market value. That is how much a reasonable buyer would pay to buy it today. Fair market value might be less than what you paid for the item, but it is the best estimate of what your asset is worth. For example, you may have paid $500 for a computer two years ago. If you sold it today, a buyer might only pay $250 for the used computer. In this case, you should assign a fair market value of $250 to the computer on your net worth statement.

You may want to use a spreadsheet like this one to set up your net worth calculation. Then you can easily update it in the future.

After you have listed all your assets, you need to list the money that you owe. These are your liabilities. You might owe money on a credit card, a car loan, or a mortgage. You might have borrowed money from a friend or parent.

Assets	Value
Savings account	$1,000
Savings bonds	$500
Cash on hand	$125
Computer	$250
MP3 player	$100
Car	$15,000
Jewelry	$400
Total Assets	$17,375

Liabilities	Value
Credit card balance – Visa	$150
Credit card balance – American Express	$100
Student loan	$1,000
Car loan	$13,000
Unpaid bills	$200
Total Liabilities	**$14,450**

Once you have listed everything, add up your assets. Then total your liabilities. Your net worth is the difference between your total assets and total liabilities.

Calculate your net worth as follows:

Total assets - Total liabilities = Net worth

If your assets are greater than your liabilities, you have a positive net worth. In our example, net worth is $17,375 - $14,450 = $2.925.

If your liabilities are higher than your assets, your net worth is negative. You owe more than you own. Do not be discouraged if your net worth is negative. Now that you know where you stand, you can use the information from your net worth statement to start planning your path to smart savings and financial planning.

Checking In

Now that you have calculated your net worth, it will only take you a few minutes to update your calculations. You can use

If you find that you have not made progress toward your financial goals when you update your net worth statement, you may need to brainstorm ways you can change your spending and saving habits.

this tool to check in periodically on how you are doing on your financial goals. Net worth statements can be recalculated on a monthly, quarterly, or annual basis. Seeing the progress that you are making on your financial goals and watching your net worth grow can be rewarding.

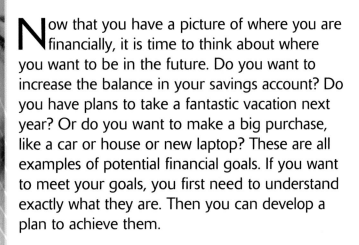

CHAPTER 2

Setting Financial Goals

Now that you have a picture of where you are financially, it is time to think about where you want to be in the future. Do you want to increase the balance in your savings account? Do you have plans to take a fantastic vacation next year? Or do you want to make a big purchase, like a car or house or new laptop? These are all examples of potential financial goals. If you want to meet your goals, you first need to understand exactly what they are. Then you can develop a plan to achieve them.

Importance of Setting Goals

Goals are the building blocks of your financial success. They provide motivation to keep you moving on the path to achieving what you want financially. Without specific goals, it is easy to forget why you need to stick to a budget instead of splurging on the latest pair of designer jeans.

Many people make the mistake of focusing too much on daily expenses and losing sight of long-term goals. Without an eye to the future, daily expenses can quickly take up all of your available money. If you spend all of your money

each month, you will never have enough to save and invest for the future. Specific goals will help you focus on what you want to achieve. A plan to meet goals can help you ignore distractions that may threaten to sidetrack you along the way.

Decide What You Want

The beginning of every financial plan is a wish list. A wish list includes everything that you want to achieve, from buying a boat to paying for college. To make a wish list, think about what you want. Some people want to save for a large purchase, like a television, car, or computer. Others want to pay for home improvements, pay off a loan, or save for a vacation.

One of your financial goals may be to save enough money for a dream vacation. These teens are enjoying a trip to the beach with their savings.

Some people dream of saving enough money to stay home with their children or retire early.

Goals are different for each person. They should be what you want, not what someone has told you to want. You need to desire a goal enough to make sacrifices for it now so that you can enjoy your reward in the future. Although your goals should be realistic, do not be afraid to stretch a little for something that seems just out of reach. Working hard to achieve a goal will make the reward sweeter.

The best goals are specific. Instead of saying that you want to save more money, be clear about why you want to save and what you want to achieve. Do you want to purchase a house? Try setting a specific goal to put aside $100 per month into a house fund. Do you want to pay for college? A specific goal would be to contribute $50 each month to a college fund. If you want to pay down outstanding debt, set a goal to pay $75 toward that debt each month. The more specific you are with your goals, the easier it will be to develop a workable plan to meet them.

Put It in Writing

Once you have chosen your goals, put them in writing. For many people, seeing a goal in black and white makes it more real. Although writing it down seems simple, this step allows you to take your goals more seriously. As a result, you may put more effort into achieving them. Writing it down also creates a record that holds you accountable to your financial plans.

When writing down a goal, describe it in detail. Include how much money and time it will take to achieve the goal. For example, if your goal is to buy a new car, be as specific as you can about the type of car you visualize yourself driving. Do some research into current car prices for vehicles like the one

Some teens feel more comfortable using a pen and paper to write down their financial goals. Others may choose to write their goals in an electronic diary on a computer.

you plan to buy. Consider if you plan to buy the car new or used. Then set a deadline for achieving your goal. Giving yourself a date creates a sense of urgency that helps increase your focus when working toward a goal.

Long-Term vs. Short-Term Goals

At first, most of your goals may be long-term. Long-term goals are defined as those that will take five or more years to achieve. Working toward something that is five or more years away can make it difficult to stay focused. To help, see if you can break down each of your long-term goals into shorter,

Time Value of Money

The time value of money means that a dollar today is worth more than a dollar in the future. This occurs because today's dollar can be invested and earn interest. To illustrate the time value of money, consider the following example. If someone offers to pay you $1,000 today or $1,300 in five years, which should you take? Using the time value of money concept, you can calculate that $1,000 today invested with a 6 percent interest rate would be worth $1,467 in five years. In this case, you would be better off taking the $1,000 payment today and investing it. The time value of money is the reason why it is better to receive $1 today than $1 tomorrow.

more manageable short-term chunks. For example, you may have a long-term goal of saving $20,000 over seven years for a down payment on a house. You can break this longer goal into smaller, short-term goals of putting $1,000 each year or $100 per month into a house fund. That way, you can celebrate the success of reaching short-term goals each month while still progressing toward the long-term goal.

Other financial goals may be short-term or medium-term. Short-term goals should take approximately one year or less to achieve. Medium-term goals stretch a bit longer, between one to four years. Although these goals are shorter in duration, you can use the same idea of making them more manageable by breaking them into smaller monthly chunks. For example, if

you are saving $1,000 to buy a new laptop, make a monthly goal to save $100 toward the new computer.

Important Goal: An Emergency Fund

One financial goal that many people have is to build an emergency fund. An emergency fund provides a safety net for job loss, illness, or other unexpected expenses. Maybe your car breaks down and you have unplanned repair costs. You might get sick and incur expensive medical bills. If the unthinkable happens and you lose your job, an emergency fund will provide money to pay bills for several months while you search for your next job.

You may need to use your emergency funds to pay for unexpected medical bills and prescriptions when you get sick.

Most financial advisers suggest that you have three to six months' worth of living expenses saved in your emergency fund. You should be able to quickly and easily access the money when you need it.

Evaluate Progress Regularly

It is important to revisit goals regularly. Each month, take the time to review goals and track your progress against them. Short-term goals should be reviewed at least monthly, while long-term goals can be reviewed less frequently. This review helps you see where you are succeeding and where you are having problems meeting your goals. If you identify problem areas, you can investigate why this is happening. Then you can make adjustments, whether it means trying a little harder to save or adjusting the period on your goal to make it more realistic.

When you review, you may realize that your goals have changed. You may no longer want to buy a boat, or you may have decided to attend a less expensive college. A good financial plan is flexible enough to adjust as your wants and circumstances change. Make the necessary changes in your goals and revise your plans accordingly.

If you have trouble staying motivated to save, focus on the benefits of achieving your goals. Think about how good it will feel to drive a new car or go on vacation. If you remind yourself of these benefits often, it will be easier to make sacrifices today in order to achieve goals in the future.

CHAPTER 3

Preparing a Budget

Once your goals are in place, the next step is to understand where your money comes from (income) and where it goes (expenses). A budget is a tool that you can use to list all your income and expenses. Once you see where you earn and spend money, you can find opportunities to save money. You can set targets for spending so that you can meet savings goals. Setting up a budget and sticking to it may be a lot of work, but it is an important part of meeting your financial goals.

Trying to save money without a budget will usually end in failure. Many people spend more money than they realize. Some even spend more money than they make, causing them to go into debt. Spending without knowing how much money you have available is usually the main cause of these problems. Creating a budget that tells you exactly how much money you have (or do not have) to spend keeps you in control of your financial choices. This knowledge will help you decide how you want to spend or save your money.

Making a Budget Worksheet

You can set up a budget in a simple worksheet, either on the computer or on paper. Good budgets include income, expenses, and savings categories. The worksheet categories should be detailed enough to be useful, but not so detailed that it takes hours to complete the worksheet each month.

To begin, think about all of your income sources. Where does your money come from? Do you earn wages at a job, get a weekly allowance, or earn interest from an investment? Some typical income sources are:

- Wages
- Bonuses
- Gifts
- Child support or alimony
- Rental income
- Interest income
- Dividend income
- Other income

Next, think about how you spend your money. What are your living expenses? Do you live in an apartment? If so, you probably have rent and utility payments. Do you own a car? Make sure to include car payments, gas, and insurance as part of your expenses. When building the expense categories on your budget, consider your personal habits and the things you like to do, such as traveling, golfing, or crafting.

Some expenses are fixed. Fixed expenses like rent or student loan payments are about the same every month. Other expenses are variable, such as clothing purchases or restaurant meals. These expenses fluctuate based on your spending choices.

A careful review of the checks that you have written in the past six months can help you find expenses that you forgot to list on your budget worksheet.

When listing your expenses, do not forget to include expenses that you do not pay every month. These expenses might be annual insurance payments, subscriptions, holiday or birthday gifts, or tuition payments. You may want to set aside a monthly amount for these items in your budget. Then when it is time to pay for them, you will have the money available.

Some typical expense categories are:

- Mortgage or rent
- Utilities
- Student loan payments
- Debt payments
- Credit card payments
- Restaurant meals
- Insurance
- Clothing and shoes
- Entertainment—movies, concerts
- Medical expenses
- Gifts and donations
- Travel expenses
- Car expenses—gas, maintenance
- Interest expense
- Taxes
- Retirement contributions
- Savings contributions
- Miscellaneous expenses

Once you have identified your income and expense categories, you may want to use a spreadsheet to set up your budget. Then you can easily update the spreadsheet each month.

A sample budget worksheet:

Income	Value
Wages	$3,000
Interest income	$100
Total income	**$3,100**
Expenses	
Rent	$1,200
Car payment	$300
Taxes	$500
School loan	$300
Insurance	$200
Eating out	$200
Clothing	$100
Misc. expenses	$200
Savings	$100
Total expenses	$3,100
Net income	$0

As you use your budget each month, you will see how it fits within your lifestyle. Some people may prefer a simpler budget, while others want to understand their expenses in detail. If the budget is too detailed, you can combine some categories. If you find that you want to know more about a large category, you can break it into more detailed lines on your budget. Either way, the result should be that your budget becomes a tool that provides valuable and useful information,

Using a computer can help you efficiently track expenses each month. You may be able to download expense activity from your bank account and credit cards directly into a computer program or worksheet.

but does not become so tedious that you dread completing it each month.

What Happens to Your Money?

Now that you have identified the categories in your budget, track your income, expenses, and savings for a few months to get a good understanding of your sources and uses of money. Knowing exactly how much money you have each month and where it goes is a critical piece of information. It will help you set realistic goals when you create a spending and savings plan.

To track monthly income and expenses, you will need to gather several sources of information. Collect your pay stubs, bank statements, credit card bills, receipts, and other bills for several weeks. Use a month's worth of pay stubs to estimate your monthly income before taxes. Add any other sources of monthly income to your budget worksheet. This will give you an estimate of how much money you have available each month.

Next you will need to track where you have spent your money. Using bills, credit card statements, pay stubs, your check register, and receipts, track the expenses in your budget. Go through all of your documents, and assign each expense to a budget category. When all expenses have been assigned, total each category and complete the expense portion of the budget worksheet. For categories that have annual or nonre-curring payments like insurance, take the amount of your annual bill and divide it by twelve months. Enter the monthly amount into the budget worksheet.

Tracking cash expenses is another important part of under-standing your expenses. Many people withdraw money from their bank accounts but cannot remember where they spent

Personal Finance Software

A spreadsheet can do a good job of tracking a simple budget with a few income and expense categories. As budgets get more detailed, you may want to consider using one of the many types of personal finance software available. These programs can be automated to make the job of updating your budget each month easier and less time-consuming. You can find personal finance software anywhere computer software is sold, such as office supply stores and computer stores. Quicken is one of the most popular personal finance software programs.

With personal finance software, you will be able to analyze your income and expenses in many ways and print out graphs and reports from your computer. The software enables you to create budgets and then compare budget targets to actual amounts by categories. You can also enter detailed information about your assets, liabilities, investments, and debts to create net worth statements. For some people, this is the most effective way to manage their finances and keep saving on track.

There are also many Web sites designed to help you keep track of your budget. Many of them are free to access. Just be sure to check around to make sure that they are legitimate before plugging in any personal information.

the cash. To understand where you spend cash, save the receipt or record the expense in a notebook each time you pay for something. Then enter this information into your budget worksheet. It may seem tedious to save a receipt for a tiny expense, but over time it will provide you with valuable information about your spending habits.

Once you start tracking how you spend your money, you may be surprised. Many people think they know where their money goes each month. Yet when they actually track each dollar spent, they find that small cash expenditures add up to big expenses each month. When you think about it, a $1 candy

Many teens do not realize how much money they spend eating out with friends until they begin to track their expenses. Knowing where your money goes can help you make smart spending choices.

bar from the vending machine each day adds up to almost $400 a year. Over five years, that multiplies to almost $2,000!

Recognize Spending Patterns

Recording and reviewing your monthly expenses is a good way to recognize your spending patterns. Do you have a weakness for new clothes at the mall or Friday-night dinners at the hot new restaurant in town? Seeing how much money is flowing out the door can help you curb impulse buys the next time you are at the store.

In addition, recognizing where you spend your money can help you spot areas where you can save painlessly. Do you spend $10 to buy lunch every day at the food court near your work? Packing a lunch from home four days a week could save $40 a week. Making your morning coffee at home instead of stopping at the local doughnut shop could save over $1 a day, which can add up to almost $400 a year.

CHAPTER 4

Make a Savings Plan

Saving money does not happen by accident. You save by creating a plan to make smart purchases and spend less money. Now that you have tracked where your money comes from and where it goes on a budget worksheet, you have the information you need to create a savings plan.

A savings plan is an important part of financial planning. It identifies where you can cut costs to increase savings. It helps you make smart buying decisions and avoid impulse spending. A savings plan is the roadmap that shows you the path to take to get from where you are today to meeting your financial goals in the future.

Set Spending Targets

The first step in creating a savings plan is to set spending targets for each of your expenses. Using the knowledge that you learned when creating a budget worksheet, you can estimate how much money you will need each month by expense.

Setting realistic spending targets is important. Unrealistic targets set you up to fail and provide

This teen is saving money by eating breakfast at home instead of spending money at the local coffee shop. Over time, this small savings will add up and help him reach his financial goals faster.

no incentive to stick with your spending plan. If you consistently spend $100 per month on restaurants, it is unrealistic to expect that you will not spend any money eating out next month. If you want to reduce the amount of money you spend on meals, a more realistic target that gives you a chance to succeed may be lowering the expense to $50 for the first few months.

When making your spending plan, do not forget to pay yourself. Yes, make paying yourself one of your expense categories. This helps make savings a priority each month, just like paying your rent or car payment.

Look for Opportunities to Save

When creating your spending plan, keep an eye out for opportunities to trim your expenses and save more money. At first, you may think that there is no wiggle room in your plan and you need to spend every dollar that you have listed. Yet with enough effort, nearly everyone can find some savings in their spending plan.

Variable expenses are usually the easiest place to cut expenses and find savings. Could you cut back on eating out to once or twice a month? What if you changed the Friday-night restaurant dinner to a rotating potluck dinner with friends? Do you stop at the local bagel place each morning for breakfast? How much could you save if you ate breakfast at home three mornings a week?

You could also save money by buying used instead of new. Some consignment stores or secondhand stores (like Goodwill or the Salvation Army) offer trendy clothes at a fraction of the prices at malls. Scour online sites like eBay, Freecycle, and Craigslist or local classified ads for

items like exercise equipment, sporting equipment, furniture, clothing, or electronics. Buying used, you can often get a great bargain on an item that is as good as new.

Although it might be harder, you can also find opportunities to save in your fixed expenses. Your car payment may be a set amount each month, but do you really need that expensive gas-guzzler? If you trade it in for a less expensive, more fuel-efficient vehicle, not only will you save each month with a lower car payment, but you will also be paying less for gas and car insurance. To find potential savings, evaluate each of your fixed expenses and determine if there are any ways you could cut back. You may be able to move to a less expensive apartment and save money on rent. To reduce insurance payments, see if the insurance company will give you a discount if you bundle your home and car policies with it. Moving into a smaller, less-expensive apartment today may help you save faster for a down payment on your dream house. For each sacrifice you make now, you will be one step closer to achieving your financial goals.

Each dollar that you reduce expenses can be used to increase your savings. Are you saving enough to meet your goals? If not, reexamine your expenses and see if you can make additional cuts. Do not be discouraged if you do not have any extra money to save at first. By developing a realistic budget and savings plan and sticking to them, you will create money for savings over time.

As you get comfortable finding ways to reduce your expenses and find savings, you may find yourself questioning every dollar that you spend to make sure it is really worth it. With this cost-cutting focus, you will enjoy watching your savings build each month!

Simple Ideas to Save Money

Here are some easy ways to cut back on expenses and save more money for your financial goals:

- Make a shopping list before you hit the store and stick to it.

- Set a spending limit for impulse buys, for example $5 to $10.

- Limit the amount of cash that you carry and leave credit cards at home.

- Research large purchases before you buy. Compare prices online at different stores. Ask the store to match a lower price at its competitor.

- Embrace used items instead of new. Visit consignment and secondhand shops. Borrow from the library.

- Keep track of little things—magazines and packs of gum can add up over a month or year.

Monitor Progress Monthly

You have analyzed your budget, created a savings plan, and entered everything into a budget worksheet. Now what? All the work you have done will not mean anything unless you hold yourself accountable each month for your spending and

savings decisions. That means you need to monitor your progress against your budget and plan on a regular basis.

Each month, fill out your budget spreadsheet and compare your actual income, expenses, and savings against the targets

By learning how to maintain his car and do minor repairs himself, this teen has reduced his expenses and is saving the money he would have had to pay to an auto mechanic.

in your savings plan. Did you earn as much as you thought you would? If not, where was the difference? On your expenses, did you meet the targets or did you overspend? Use what you learn to refine your budget and make it a better tool to manage your money.

Identify and Plug Spending Leaks

As you monitor your actual spending against targets each month, you may be able to identify patterns of spending leaks or unintended purchases. You may have a weakness for buying sodas at the convenience store or downloading the latest music on iTunes or purchasing the latest video game. As you identify the reasons you have overspent in certain categories, think about why you exceeded the targets. Was it something unavoidable, like replacing a flat tire on your car? Or was it an impulse buy that you did not need? Understanding where and when spending leaks occur can help you better plan and stick to your budget in the future.

Focus on Savings

Making savings a priority will help you achieve your goals. Paying yourself as an expense category is one way to focus on savings. You can also prioritize saving by setting up a separate savings account. A barrier between your savings and the cash you need for day-to-day expenses prevents you from unintentionally dipping into your savings for impulse buys. It also makes it easier to see your savings grow each month.

Another way to focus on savings is to automate them. Many employers have the ability to split the direct deposit of your paycheck into two or more bank accounts. If your employer allows it, designate a set percentage or dollar amount of your

Many teens make savings a priority by setting aside a regular amount from each paycheck and depositing it into a savings account each week or month.

wages and have it automatically deposited into a separate savings account. It is much easier to save if it happens automatically each month. You can also automate savings by setting up a monthly bank transfer from your checking to your savings account. You can even write yourself a check from your checking to your savings account each month, as if you were paying a bill to yourself. Any way you accomplish it, making savings an automatic monthly occurrence is a big step toward increasing your savings.

Where to Keep Your Money

As your money grows, you will have to decide where to keep it. Banks offer several types of accounts that many people use for savings:

- Savings accounts: A savings account usually holds money for long-term needs. Banks will pay you interest to keep your money in a savings account and leave it there. Money put into a savings account is easy to access when you need it. Usually, it can be withdrawn without penalty.
- Interest-paying checking accounts: Some banks offer interest-paying checking accounts. These accounts allow you to write checks, and the bank pays you interest on the balance that you keep in the account. The interest on these accounts is usually less than the interest a bank pays on a savings account.
- Certificates of deposit (CDs): Many banks offer a type of investment called a certificate of deposit, or CD. When you buy a CD, you agree to invest your money with the bank for a specific period of time. The bank agrees to pay you a specific rate of interest on the money you invest. You can purchase CDs in a variety of durations and

amounts. The longer the duration of the CD and the larger the investment, the higher interest rate the bank will pay. The interest paid on CDs is usually higher than savings accounts and interest-paying checking accounts. However, if you need to take your money out of the CD before the end of its duration, you will have to pay a penalty.

• Money market accounts: A money market account is a type of savings account offered by some banks and investment firms. The interest paid on money market accounts is usually higher than that paid on interest-paying checking accounts.

Myths & Facts

Myth   I cannot afford to save money.

Fact   Everyone can save something each week or month, no matter how small. Scour your spending and identify expenses that are no longer needs, but have become habits. Simple strategies, such as packing a bag lunch, making coffee-to-go at home, and quitting smoking, are all ways to trim the fat from your expenses and save money.

Myth   Saving means I will have to sacrifice the things that I want.

Fact   Saving is the roadmap to achieving your financial goals, the items that are really important to you. Saving and a spending plan will show you what you can afford to buy now and still make progress toward the things you want in the future. As you achieve your financial goals, you will not go without. You will enjoy more.

Myth   Saving money only makes sense if you have something specific that you want to buy.

Fact   As much as you plan, unexpected expenses will come up from time to time. You never know when an emergency will arise and you need cash on hand to pay for car repairs or medical bills. Maybe your favorite band will add a nearby city to their summer tour. If you have money saved for unexpected events, you will be able to pay for these events without jeopardizing your financial plans.

Chapter 5

Financial Planning for Tomorrow

No matter what your age, it is never too early to begin planning for your financial future. Your long-term financial goals may include college, home ownership, and retirement. You may have started saving in a piggy bank, but as your goals get bigger and your cash increases, you may want to think about the best place for your savings.

Checking or Savings Accounts

There are many good reasons to keep your money in a checking or savings account. One of the most important is safety. Money in the bank is better protected against loss or theft. The federal government insures deposits at many banks. Insured banks protect your account for up to $100,000 or $250,000 for retirement accounts. Banks also pay interest on your savings, which allows your money to grow over time. Banks also offer easy access to your money when you need it. No matter what day or time it is, you can usually withdraw money from your bank account using an automated teller machine (ATM).

When using an ATM, make sure no one can see your PIN. With your PIN, thieves can access your account and steal your savings.

Savings Bonds

U.S. Savings Bonds are debt securities that are issued by the federal government. Many people find them an easy and safe way to save for the future. They are considered one of the safest investments because they are backed by the federal government.

As of January 1, 2012, you can purchase savings bonds online through the U.S. Treasury. You can buy a bond for as little as $25. These bonds are sold at face value, meaning you will pay $25 for a $25 bond. You will earn interest on the bond, which will be issued electronically to the account you designate. One thing to consider is when you think you might need to use your savings. If you redeem the bond in the first five years after buying it, you will be penalized by having to forfeit the most recent three months of interest. If you redeem your bond after five years, there is no penalty.

401(k) Plans

If investing for retirement is one of your financial goals, consider saving in a 401(k) plan set up by your employer. Employees contribute up to a certain percentage of their salary to the plan. Most company 401(k) plans offer several stock, bond, and money market funds in which employees can invest their money.

The employee's contribution to a 401(k) account is made in pretax dollars, which means it is not taxed by the federal government before it is invested in the 401(k) plan. In addition, any interest or earnings that your investments make in the 401(k) account accumulate tax-free. You will pay taxes, however, when you withdraw the money in retirement. You may be in a lower tax bracket at that time and have to pay a lower tax rate than you paid when you were working.

Hidden Costs—Bank Fees

Sometimes your bank can be a source of hidden costs that quickly add up to large expenses. Banks charge customers a variety of fees, many of which you may not realize you are paying. Some banks charge a fee if a customer's account drops below a certain minimum amount. Many banks charge fees when customers use nonbranch ATMs. Overdraft charges are some of the most costly bank fees, when you accidentally write a check for more money than you have in your checking account.

Many people accept bank fees without question, yet there are ways to minimize them. Find out if your account has a minimum balance requirement. If you do not have enough money to meet the minimum consistently, consider changing to an account without a minimum. Plan ahead on ATM withdrawals to make sure that you use your bank's fee-free machines. To eliminate costly overdraft charges, ask if your bank has overdraft protection available. That way, if you bounce a check, the bank will automatically transfer money from your savings account to cover the check, saving you the fee.

Another benefit to saving in a 401(k) plan is that many employers will match, dollar for dollar, a portion of your contribution. This money also goes into an employee's 401(k) savings account. A 401(k) employer match helps your retirement savings grow at a faster rate.

It is important to recognize that 401(k) savings should be for the long-term. If you need to withdraw money from a 401(k) account before you are 59 1/2 years old, you will pay a 10 percent penalty on your withdrawal, plus any taxes owed.

IRA Accounts

Unlike 401(k) plans, which are sponsored by a company, an IRA (individual retirement account) can be opened by an individual. As of 2011, the amount you can contribute to an IRA each year is $5,000 ($6,000 annually if you are fifty years old or older).

There are two types of IRAs: traditional IRAs and Roth IRAs. In a traditional IRA, your contributions are pretax, or subtracted from your earnings before you pay taxes. In addition, any earnings that you make on the money in your IRA account are also tax-free. Once you withdraw the money from the account, you will pay taxes on your withdrawals. For people who expect to earn less money and have a lower tax rate when they retire, saving money for retirement in an IRA will help them save money on taxes.

Unlike a traditional IRA, the money invested in a Roth IRA is taxed before it goes into the account. Any earnings in the Roth IRA, however, are not taxable. When you withdraw the money, you will not have to pay taxes on it. If you expect to be earning more money and have a higher tax rate when you retire, a Roth IRA might be a better choice for retirement savings.

Investing for the Future

Once you are on the road toward your long-term financial goals, you may consider different investment options to help

Selecting a variety of stocks and bonds to invest in will diversify your risk. If one or more of your investments declines, diversification will help protect your money.

Ten Great Questions to Ask
a Professional Financial Adviser

1 How much money should I keep in an emergency fund?

2 Where should I put my savings—in a savings account, CD, savings bond, or a combination of all three?

3 How can I get a better interest rate on my savings?

4 What bank savings accounts are paying the best interest right now?

5 What percentage of my wages should I contribute to my 401(k) plan each month?

6 Should I open an IRA account? Traditional or Roth?

7 How often should I review my budget?

8 What categories are important to identify and track in my budget?

9 Where are areas that I could identify more savings in my spending plan?

10 Where is the best place to put money that I plan to use in a few years for college?

grow your savings to reach your goals. There are a number of investments available:

- **Bonds:** Bonds are a loan to a company or government. When you buy a bond, you are paid interest at regular intervals.
- **Stocks:** A stock is a share of a company. Stocks are sold in various stock markets, usually through a stockbroker. As the value of a company increases, the value of your share of stock will also increase.
- **Mutual funds:** Mutual funds are a type of investment in which many people combine their money to buy an assortment of stocks. Buying shares in a mutual fund is really like investing in a variety of companies without having to buy shares of each one separately.

Risk vs. Reward

The attraction of investing in bonds, stocks, and mutual funds is strong. Many people have made a lot of money very quickly by picking the right investments for their savings. Yet investing has risk. There is no guarantee that you will earn money on an investment. Sometimes you may lose money. When you buy a share of stock for $20, it could increase in value to $60, making $40 in profit. On the other hand, that same share of stock could decrease in value to $0, leaving you with nothing and losing your entire investment. Often the riskier an investment is, the higher its potential reward.

When evaluating your savings and investments, consider how much risk you are willing to take. You should consider these three factors:

Teens who start saving early have a better chance of meeting their long-term financial goals than people who start saving later in life. Plan and save now. You'll be happy you did!

- **Age:** A younger person has more time to earn back any money lost and can usually tolerate more risky investments.
- **Purpose:** What are you planning to use the money for? If you will need it in the next few years for college tuition or a new car, you will want to invest in a very safe investment like CDs so that you do not lose any of your principal.
- **Personality:** Some people like to take risks. Others do not. What is your risk personality? If taking risks with your money sets your stomach churning every time you think about it, keep your investments in safer choices.

Glossary

balance The amount of money currently in an account.

bond A promise from a company or government to pay a certain amount on a certain date.

budget A plan for how to spend and save money.

certificate of deposit (CD) A type of savings in which money is deposited for a certain period of time to earn a specific interest rate.

checking account A bank account that allows a person to withdraw money, pay bills, or make purchases by writing checks.

compound interest The interest earned on both the original amount and any previous interest added to the balance.

deposit To put money into.

expense A good or service that people pay for.

fixed expense An expense that stays the same and must be paid from month to month, like rent.

income Money earned for doing work or received from savings, investments, or gifts.

individual retirement account (IRA) A type of investment account that provides tax advantages to encourage people to save for retirement.

interest Money that banks pay for using funds deposited into accounts.

investing The risking of money and time to get more money in return.

mutual fund An investment run by professionals in which people pool their money to buy stocks, bonds, and other items.

net worth The total assets minus total liabilities of an individual or a company.

principal The sum of money put into an investment.

redeem To exchange for money.

savings account A bank account in which money is deposited for safekeeping.

savings bond A bond issued by the federal government sold at face value.

stock An investment in the ownership of a company.

variable expense An expense that varies from month to month.

For More Information

Canadian Foundation for Economic Education
110 Eglinton Avenue West, Suite 201
Toronto, ON M4R 1A3
Canada
(888) 570-7610
Web site: http://www.cfee.org
The Canadian Foundation for Economic Education offers
information and educational resources for teens regarding
money, personal finance, and entrepreneurship.

Consumer Federation of America
1620 I Street NW, Suite 100
Washington, DC 20006
(202) 387-6121
Web site: http://www.consumerfed.org
The Consumer Federation of America is an advocacy, research,
and education organization that provides information
and resources on personal finances, including money
management and budgeting.

Federal Deposit Insurance Corporation (FDIC)
Consumer Response Center
2345 Grand Boulevard, Suite 100
Kansas City, MO 64108-2638
(800) 378-9581
Web site: http://www.fdic.gov
The FDIC insures bank accounts. Its Web site also provides a variety
of information related to banking and the state of banks.

Financial Literacy and Education Commission
U.S. Department of the Treasury

1500 Pennsylvania Avenue NW
Washington, DC 20220
(888) MY-MONEY [696-6639]
Web site: http://www.mymoney.gov
The Financial Literacy and Education Commission offers a
    variety of information on money management and
    budgeting.

Financial Planners Standards Council
902 - 375 University Avenue
Toronto, ON M5G 2J5
Canada
(416) 593-8587
Web site: http://www.fpsccanada.org
The Financial Planners Standards Council provides information
    on financial planning, personal finance, choosing a financial
    planner, and more.

Jump$tart
919 Eighteenth Street NW, Suite 300
Washington, DC 20006
(888) 45-EDUCATE [453-3822]
Web site: http://www.jumpstartcoalition.org
Jump$tart is a national coalition of organizations dedicated to
    improving the financial literacy of prekindergarten
    through college-age youth by providing advocacy,
    research, standards, and educational resources.

Junior Achievement
One Education Way
Colorado Springs, CO 80906
Web site: http://studentcenter.ja.org

Junior Achievement offers information and games to help
youth learn about personal finance and managing their
money.

National Association of Personal Financial Advisors (NAPFA)
3250 North Arlington Heights Road, Suite 109
Arlington Heights, IL 60004
(84) 483-5400
Web site: http://www.napfa.org
The NAPFA is a professional association of financial advisers.
Its Web site provides a variety of educational materials
related to personal finance and investing.

Web Sites

Due to the changing nature of Internet links, Rosen Publishing
has developed an online list of Web sites related to the subject
of this book. This site is updated regularly. Please use this link
to access the list:

http://www.rosenlinks.com/GSM/Save

For Further Reading

Berg, David W., and Meg Green. *Savings and Investments*. New York, NY: Rosen Central, 2012.

Bijlefeld, Marjolijn, and Sharon K. Zoumbaris. *Teen Guide to Personal Financial Management*. Westport, CT: Greenwood, 2000.

Butler, Tamsen. *The Complete Guide to Personal Finance for Teenagers and College Students*. Ocala, FL: Atlantic Publishing Group, 2010.

Chatzky, Jean Sherman, and Erwin Haya. *Not Your Parents' Money Book: Making, Saving, and Spending Your Own Money*. New York, NY: Simon & Schuster for Young Readers, 2010.

Collins, Robyn, and Kimberly Spinks Burleson. *Prepare to Be a Teen Millionaire*. Deerfield Beach, FL: HCI, 2008.

Denega, Danielle. *Smart Money: How to Manage Your Cash*. London, England: Franklin Watts, 2008.

Donovan, Sandra. *Budgeting Smarts: How to Set Goals, Save Money, Spend Wisely, and More*. Minneapolis, MN: Twenty-First Century, 2012.

Einspruch, Andrew. *Managing Money*. Mankato, MN: Smart Apple Media, 2012.

Fradin, Dennis B., and Judith Bloom. *Saving*. Tarrytown, NY: Marshall Cavendish Benchmark, 2011.

Freedman, Jeri. *First Bank Account and First Investments Smarts*. New York, NY: Rosen Publishing, 2010.

Hamilton, Brian. *90 Day Money Challenge: Boot Camp for Financial Fitness*. Baltimore, MD: Gorsuch Graphics, LLC, 2011.

Hamilton, Jill. *Money Management*. Detroit, MI: Greenhaven, 2009.

Hollander, Barbara. *Managing Money*. Chicago, IL: Heineman, 2008.

Kiyosaki, Robert T. *Rich Dad Poor Dad for Teens: The Secrets About Money—That You Don't Learn in School!* Scottsdale, AZ: Plata Publishing, 2012.

Kwas, Susan Estelle. *It's a Money Thing!: A Girl's Guide to Managing Money.* San Francisco, CA: Chronicle, 2008.

Minden, Cecilia. *Smart Shopping.* Ann Arbor, MI: Cherry Lake Publishing, 2008.

Minden, Cecilia. *What Is Money?* Ann Arbor, MI: Cherry Lake Publishing, 2009.

Peterson, Judy Monroe. *First Budget Smarts.* New York, NY: Rosen Publishing, 2010.

Sember, Brette McWhorter. *The Everything Kids' Money Book: Earn It, Save It, and Watch It Grow!* Avon, MA: Adams Media, 2008.

Vickers, Rebecca. *101 Ways to Be Smart About Money.* Chicago, IL: Raintree, 2012.

Bibliography

CNNMoney. "Banking and Saving Basics." Retrieved March 10, 2012 (http://money.cnn.com/magazines/moneymag/money101/lesson3/index.htm).

CNNMoney. "Making a Budget." Retrieved March 10, 2012 (http://money.cnn.com/magazines/moneymag/money101/lesson2/index.htm).

CNNMoney. "Setting Priorities." Retrieved March 10, 2012 (http://money.cnn.com/magazines/moneymag/money101/lesson1/index.htm).

Cramer, Jim. *Real Money: Sane Investing in an Insane World.* New York, NY: Simon & Schuster, 2005.

Fowles, Debby. *The Everything Personal Finance in Your 20s & 30s Book.* 2nd ed. Avon, MA: Adams Media, 2008.

Inflation Data.com. "Historical Inflation." Retrieved March 23, 2012 (http://inflationdata.com/inflation/Inflation_Rate/HistoricalInflation.aspx).

Internal Revenue Service. "401 (k) Plans." Retrieved March 15, 2012 (http://www.irs.gov/retirement/article/0,,id=120298,00.html).

Internal Revenue Service. "Individual Retirement Arrangements (IRAs)." Retrieved March 15, 2012 (http://www.irs.gov/retirement/article/0,,id=226255,00.html).

Kansas, Dave. *The Wall Street Journal Guide to the New Rules of Personal Finance.* New York, NY: HarperCollins, 2011.

Kobliner, Beth. *Get a Financial Life: Personal Finance in Your Twenties and Thirties.* New York, NY: Fireside Books, 2009.

Orman, Suze. *The Money Book for the Young, Fabulous & Broke.* New York, NY: Riverhead Books, 2005.

SaveAndInvest.org. "Financial Basics." Retrieved March 10, 2012 (http://www.saveandinvest.org/FinancialBasics).

Index

About the Author

Carla Mooney has a B.S. in economics from the University of Pennsylvania. She has worked as a certified public accountant, director of financial reporting, and financial consultant to small businesses for more than fifteen years. Currently, she writes for young people and is the author of numerous educational books. She has been an avid saver since getting her first allowance as a young girl.

Photo Credits

Cover (right) © iStockphoto.com/PIKSEL; cover, p. 1 (top left) © iStockphoto.com/Nick M. Do; cover, p. 1 (center left) © iStockphoto.com/Matej Pribelsky; cover, p. 1 (bottom left) © iStockphoto.com/catenarymedia; cover, p. 1 (background) © iStockphoto.com/Dean Turner; pp. 4–5 Monkey Business Images/the Agency Collection/Getty Images; pp. 7, 10, 16, 23, 33, 44 wavebreakmedia ltd/Shutterstock.com; p. 9 Goodluz/Shutterstock.com; p. 15 iStockphoto/Thinkstock; p. 17 FogStock/Thinkstock; p. 19 Gary S. Chapman/Photographer's Choice RF/Getty Images; p. 21 Patrizia Tilly/Shutterstock.com; p. 25 David Young-Wolff/PhotoEdit; p. 28 © iStockphoto.com/sturti; p. 31 Ryan McVay/Stone/Getty Images; p. 34–35 rubberball/Getty Images; p. 38 Greg Friedler/Workbook Stock/Getty Images; p. 40 Ryan McVay/Digital Vision/Thinkstock; p. 45 Juan Silva/The Image Bank/Getty Images; p. 49 Medioimages/Photodisc/Thinkstock; p. 50 iStockphoto.com/Vasiliy Kosyrev; p. 52 Creatas Images/Thinkstock; interior page graphic (arrows) © iStockphoto.com/Che McPherson.

Designer: Sam Zavieh; Editor: Bethany Bryan;
Photo Researcher: Marty Levick